Doris to Darlene

a cautionary valentine

by

Jordan Harrison

FOUNDED 1830

NEW YORK HOLLYWOOD LONDON TORONTO

SAMUELFRENCH.COM

Cover Image © Corbis Corporation

Book Copyright © 2008 by Jordan Harrison

ALL RIGHTS RESERVED

CAUTION: Professionals and amateurs are hereby warned that *DORIS TO DARLENE* is subject to a royalty. It is fully protected under the copyright laws of the United States of America, the British Commonwealth, including Canada, and all other countries of the Copyright Union. All rights, including professional, amateur, motion picture, recitation, lecturing, public reading, radio broadcasting, television and the rights of translation into foreign languages are strictly reserved. In its present form the play is dedicated to the reading public only.

The amateur live stage performance rights to *DORIS TO DARLENE* are controlled exclusively by Samuel French, Inc., and royalty arrangements and licenses must be secured well in advance of presentation. PLEASE NOTE that amateur royalty fees are set upon application in accordance with your producing circumstances. When applying for a royalty quotation and license please give us the number of performances intended, dates of production, your seating capacity and admission fee. Royalties are payable one week before the opening performance of the play to Samuel French, Inc., at 45 W. 25th Street, New York, NY 10010.

Royalty of the required amount must be paid whether the play is presented for charity or gain and whether or not admission is charged.

Stock royalty quoted upon application to Samuel French, Inc.

For all other rights than those stipulated above, apply to The William Morris Agency, LLC, 1325 Avenue of the Americas, New York, NY 10019, Attn: Don Aslan.

Particular emphasis is laid on the question of amateur or professional readings, permission and terms for which must be secured in writing from Samuel French, Inc.

Copying from this book in whole or in part is strictly forbidden by law, and the right of performance is not transferable.

Whenever the play is produced the following notice must appear on all programs, printing and advertising for the play: "Produced by special arrangement with Samuel French, Inc."

Due authorship credit must be given on all programs, printing and advertising for the play.

ISBN 978-0-573-66239-3   Printed in U.S.A.   #6923

No one shall commit or authorize any act or omission by which the copyright of, or the right to copyright, this play may be impaired.

No one shall make any changes in this play for the purpose of production.

Publication of this play does not imply availability for performance. Both amateurs and professionals considering a production are strongly advised in their own interests to apply to Samuel French, Inc., for written permission before starting rehearsals, advertising, or booking a theatre.

No part of this book may be reproduced, stored in a retrieval system, or transmitted in any form, by any means, now known or yet to be invented, including mechanical, electronic, photocopying, recording, videotaping, or otherwise, without the prior written permission of the publisher.

IMPORTANT BILLING AND CREDIT REQUIREMENTS

All producers of *DORIS TO DARLENE* must give credit to the Author of the Play in all programs distributed in connection with performances of the Play, and in all instances in which the title of the Play appears for the purposes of advertising, publicizing or otherwise exploiting the Play and/or a production. The name of the Author *must* appear on a separate line on which no other name appears, immediately following the title and *must* appear in size of type not less than fifty percent of the size of the title type.

In addition the following credit must be given in all programs and publicity information distributed in association with this piece:

Playwrights Horizons, Inc., New York City, produced the World Premiere of "Doris to Darlene" Off-Broadway in 2007. "Doris to Darlene" was written with the support of a NEA/TCG Playwright-in-Residence Grant at The Empty Space Theatre and a McKnight Advancement Grant from The Playwrights' Center.

SPECIAL NOTE ABOUT MUSIC USE

Licensees are solely responsible for obtaining formal written permission from copyright owners to use copyrighted music in the performance of this play and are strongly cautioned to do so. If no such permission is obtained by the licensee, then the licensee must use only original music that the licensee owns and controls. Licensees are solely responsible and liable for all music clearances and shall indemnify the copyright owners of the play and their licensing agent, Samuel French, Inc., against any costs, expenses, losses and liabilities arising from the use of music by licensees.

PLAYWRIGHTS HORIZONS

Tim Sanford
Artistic Director

Leslie Marcus
Managing Director

William Russo
General Manager

presents

DORIS TO DARLENE,
a cautionary valentine

A new play by

Jordan Harrison

Featuring

**de'Adre Aziza   David Chandler   Michael Crane
Laura Heisler   Tom Nelis   Tobias Segal**

Scenic Design	Costume Design	Lighting Design
Takeshi Kata	Christal Weatherly	Jane Cox
Soundscape	Original Music	Music Arrangement & Production
Darron L West	Kirsten Childs	Victor Zupanc
Press Representative	Casting	Director of Development
The Publicity Office	Alaine Alldaffer, C.S.A.	Jill Garland

Production Stage Manager
Elizabeth Moreau

Production Manager
Christopher Boll

Directed by

Les Waters

Doris to Darlene was written with the support of a NEA/TCG Playwright-in-Residence Grant at The Empty Space Theatre, Seattle, WA
Allison Narver, Artistic Director

Doris to Darlene was written with the support of a McKnight Advancement Grant from The Playwrights' Center, Minneapolis, MN
Polly Carl, Producing Artistic Director

Major support for *Doris to Darlene* was generously provided by The Blanche and Irving Laurie Foundation.

Special thanks to The Harold and Mimi Steinberg Charitable Trust for supporting new plays at Playwrights Horizons.

Special thanks to Time Warner, Inc. for its leadership support of The American Voice: New Play and Musical Theater Development at Playwrights Horizons.

CAST

Doris .... DE'ADRE AZIZA
Vic Watts .... MICHAEL CRANE

King Ludwig II .... LAURA HEISLER
Richard Wagner .... DAVID CHANDLER

The Young Man .... TOBIAS SEGAL
Mr. Campani .... TOM NELIS

Production Stage Manager .... ELIZABETH MOREAU
Assistant Stage Manager .... MARLA K. SHAFFER

CHARACTERS

Six Actors (2W, 4M.)

DORIS, a girl singer, mixed race, from 16 to 41.
VIC WATTS, a record producer, white, from 22 to 47.

RICHARD WAGNER, a composer, about 50.
LUDWIG II, King of Bavaria, 18. (To be played by a young woman.)

MR. CAMPANI, a dapper teacher, early 40s.
THE YOUNG MAN, 16.

Casting Note:
While Doris and Vic Watts age more than twenty years over the course of the play, I encourage using actors toward the young end of this spectrum.

ON THE DOUBLING

All of the principals double in smaller roles from time to time. This should feel informal, playful – their disguises are by no means complete:

Doris's GRANDMOTHER is played by the actor who plays Mr. Campani.
The RECEPTIONIST is played by the actress who plays Ludwig.
MISS LUFTUS is played by the actor who plays Wagner.
PROM DATE played by Ludwig.
TALK SHOW HOST played by Wagner.
BILLY ZIMMER played by Vic Watts.
JOURNALISTS 1 and 2 played by Mr. Campani and the Young Man.
STABLE BOY played by the Young Man.
PFORDTEN played by Doris and PFISTERMEISTER played by Vic Watts.
MAKEUP GIRL played by Ludwig.

ON THE THIRD PERSON

All of the characters have the ability to narrate the story from time to time.
"Live" dialogue is indicated in boldface, like so...

DORIS. And Doris stands there in her best dress thinking:
> **No way will Grandmother call me by some name some *man* gave me.**

I suspect that bolded and un-bolded speech shouldn't actually sound very different. This third-person narration should still be in character and should feel active, filled with the discoveries of the present moment. This isn't a story that the characters have told before – it's still happening. The third-person language can be spoken directly from one actor to another, whenever this pleases. In the production at Playwrights Horizons, there were only a few instances when the actors spoke directly to the audience (the Prologue is one example). While they sometimes faced out, the third-person narration had a somewhat more interior quality, like thoughts spoken aloud.

ON THE MUSIC

The seed of *Doris to Darlene* is ten short seconds of a seldom-heard 1966 Ronettes single called "When I Saw You," produced by Phil Spector. One of Spector's more languid songs, its lyrics are characteristically undemanding: "When I saw you / That's when I knew / I'd lose my mind over you." But at the very end, a flock of violins lifts the whole production, playing the unmistakable melody of the "Liebestod" from Wagner's Tristan und Isolde.

Although a hundred years separate them, Richard Wagner's operas and Phil Spector's girl-group songs have always been easily linked in my mind. Partly because of their enormous scope (both Wagner and Spector used an unprecedented number of instruments), and because Spector described the hits he produced, famously, as "little symphonies for the kids." But the primary reason that I connect Wagner with Spector is that I discovered them both when I was a teenager, and loved their music passionately and a little guiltily.

While *Doris to Darlene* takes place at the musical intersection of Wagner and Spector, it is not intended as a biography of either man so much as a fantasia on their music. (I've taken liberties with – and greatly condensed – Wagner's years writing the Ring cycle; Spector disappears altogether, replaced by the fictional Vic Watts, who does not seem to share the former's recent bout with infamy.) The play brings us closer, instead, to the characters who are their listeners, patrons, and protégés.

Doris has two songs in the play. The first is the top-ten hit that incorporates the most recognizable melodies from Wagner's "Liebestod." The second is the song that Vic Watts writes especially for her, a version of which they recreate live in the talk show scene. I highly recommend Kirsten Childs's compositions for the Playwrights Horizons production. If you wish to undertake your own, take your cues from the age of girl-group singles after 1960's "Will You Love Me Tomorrow" and before 1966's "River Deep - Mountain High," when girl-group pop was first daring to sound grand. The age between its naïve beginnings and its decadent death knells.

For information and use of Kirsten Child's compositions please contact John Buzzetti c/o The Gersh Agency, 41 Madison Avenue, New York, NY 10010.

ON THE STAGING

One of the first things that the director Les Waters asked me when we started working on the play together was, "Do you think that we see the settings being assembled, or do they just appear suddenly, effortlessly?" As soon as he posed the question, it seemed to me that it had to be the latter. While I don't imagine that every production will need the two scene-shifting turntables that we used at Playwrights Horizons, I think a certain fluidity is essential. It should seem as much as possible like the play crosses time and space with the ease of a single sentence. It also seems that the play demands a relatively blank canvas – because the characters are so often describing where they are, it is redundant to present a fully dressed pink office or a moonlit Bavarian terrace. Takeshi Kata's pearly gray box (with subtle pink accents) for the Playwrights Horizons production not only made the play's language necessary, it allowed us to see three different centuries in sharp relief, passing each other like ships in the night.

Because the settings are necessarily simple, the costumes end up taking on a large role in the storytelling. And here seems to be the challenge: the costumes have to be malleable as well as iconic. For instance, the actor playing Wagner has to look unmistakably like Wagner – a leonine sort of man who brings the 19th century into the theater – but he also has to morph with minimal effort into a 1960s schoolmarm and talk show host. Costume designer Christal Weatherly cunningly ensured that we could always see a hint of the six principal characters peeking through: Wagner was still visible under the knit shawl of old Miss Luftus. Even as many different characters are conjured, it's important we never lose track of the play's three elemental couples.

PROLOGUE

DORIS has a portable record player and a record album under her arm. It is an early girl-group record. The Chantels would be good, or the Shirelles.

The YOUNG MAN and KING LUDWIG II are there as well. The three young people of the play, each in the dress of a different century.

YOUNG MAN. This story is about where music comes from.

KING LUDWIG II. This story is about how you put it on paper, and how you take it back off again.

DORIS. This story is about people with music in their heads, and the people who put it there.

(Doris takes the record out of its sleeve and puts it on the record player.)

YOUNG MAN. People like to say "It's our song."
But there's lots of people with the same Our Song.

(Doris lowers the arm onto the record. We hear the scratching.)

KING LUDWIG II. Sometimes a song jumps across a century. It finds a new listener and lives again.

(The song begins.)

DORIS. This story is about:
How can you sing a song for someone you never even met?

(Doris starts to dance to the music, like a girl alone in her bedroom. The Young Man and Ludwig watch her.)

(Light shifts. Continuous into:)

Scene One

LUDWIG. Doris.

YOUNG MAN. Doris.

DORIS. Doris is sixteen and she lives with her grandmother at the edge of a big city.

YOUNG MAN. Doris is sixteen and she longs for that big city, where pop music has just been invented.

LUDWIG. Doris is sixteen and she goes to school at Harper's Gulch High, where there is no music.

DORIS. But one morning she does not go to school.

One morning she walks 'till she can't see the house.

(The actor who plays Mr. Campani plays Doris's Grandmother.)

GRANDMOTHER. She can still feel her Grandmother watching the speck of her on the horizon.

DORIS. Soon as she's out of sight she puts on her special red lipstick. She catches the number nine bus to a building downtown. The elevator stops at the penthouse and the doors open and

pink and everywhere pink and ouch, the pink!

(The Ludwig actress steps in to play the Receptionist:)

RECEPTIONIST. Welcome to High Wattage Studios. You got an appointment?

DORIS. My name is Doris and I'm here to see Mr. Vic Watts at 10 o'clock sharp.

RECEPTIONIST. *(looking straight at her)*

An appraising pause.

DORIS. Doris Unsworth?

RECEPTIONIST. *(her hand shooting out to touch Doris)*

Oh *right*, the girl from the talent contest.

DORIS. *(looking down at the hand)*

Her fingernails are pink. Same pink as the walls, the carpet, the ashtray. She must have noticed Doris staring, cuz she says:

RECEPTIONIST. **Mr. Watts likes it pink.**
Mr. Watts wants his Think Space to look like cotton candy.

DORIS. And Doris pretends to read one of the gossip rags while really she's watching the clock go 9:56, 9:57, 9:58, 9:59—

VIC WATTS. **No no no no no no no.**

(Continuous into:)

Scene Two

(Cigarette smoke drifts over the top of a tall black swivel chair. VIC WATTS *swivels around so we can see him for the first time.)*

VIC WATTS. Doris Unsworth is no *good*. Doris Unsworth doesn't *sing*. Correction: Doris Unsworth sings but her name does not. What the public wants is Doris DuPont, Delicious Doris, Doo-Wop Doris, the Duchess of Doris. Doris Duke. Doris *Day*. (All the good ideas are used up.) Doris Duvall? Doris DuPont. The public wants alliteration and by God we'll give it to them. Or do away with plain ol' Doris all together and we get something like Darlene. *Darlene* DuPont. Darlene DuPont is a girl other girls want to *be*. You're turning a funny color, Darlene.

DORIS. Doris wonders what kind of man wears aviator glasses indoors.

VIC WATTS. I never seen a black girl who blushed.

DORIS. My mother was black. My dad was from France.

VIC WATTS. Lucky for us, your face matches your voice.

DORIS. *(thinking that was flirty but not sure)* Mr. Watts?

VIC WATTS. You're a pretty girl with a pretty voice and I think we can make something of you. How does that sound, Darlene?

DORIS. And Doris stands there in her best dress thinking:
No way will Grandmother call me by some name some *man* gave me.

Scene Three

DORIS. Soon as the door closes behind her, Doris hears:

VIC WATTS. Soft strange notes needling from Vic's hi-fi, soft. And strange.

(Underneath the following, we hear the early bars of Wagner's "Liebestod." We see **KING LUDWIG II** *with* **WAGNER,** *who wears a luxurious dressing gown.)*

LUDWIG. Young King Ludwig II builds a dream palace in the mountains of Bavaria. The peasants are scandalized by the pink marble. Inside, Wagner sleeps very comfortably indeed. His sleep is quieted by the pink stone, which repels sound more effectively than all other colors.

RICHARD WAGNER. Wagner dreams of enchanted swans, and dragons, and swords with names.

LUDWIG. In the next chamber, King Ludwig dreams of taller mountains, and pinker palaces, and Wagner.

DORIS. Peeking through the keyhole, Doris sees:

VIC WATTS. Vic Watts has his eyes shut tight behind those glasses.

DORIS. Vic Watts doesn't listen to the music he makes for teenagers.

WAGNER. Vic Watts only listens to Wagner, whose music takes him far from himself. Or toward himself: he can't be sure yet.

DORIS. And Doris lets herself think a dangerous thought:

LUDWIG & WAGNER. *(whispering in Doris's ear)*
Maybe there's more to him than meets the eye.

Scene Four

VIC WATTS. Vic sends Doris back to Harper's Gulch in a long black car that smells like new.

DORIS. She makes it in time for 5th period

VIC WATTS. *(as if planting these thoughts in her head)*
But the names of European capitals swim on the blackboard while she thinks What would it be like to step off a sharp-nosed silver jet into one of those European capitals on the arm of that little Machiavelli in sunglasses? Together they'll sample the finest things of Europe:

**DORIS. The waffles of Belgium,
The Black Forest cakes,
The fries of France!**

MISS LUFTUS. Doris barely notices when old Miss Luftus asks her a question.

DORIS. Huh?

MISS LUFTUS. Doris, perhaps you can daydream the capital of Luxembourg for us?

DORIS. Doris turns the color of the pink walls at High Wattage Studios.
The boys in the back row lock eyes, as if to say:

EVERYONE. *(as students)* **Who ever saw a black girl turn pink.**

DORIS. Doris walks home from school. Glad to be home.

VIC WATTS. Wait.

DORIS. *(not hearing him)* Like she's been somewhere dangerous and now she's back safe.

VIC WATTS & MISS LUFTUS. Wait!

DORIS. Back safe with a secret. Hand on the doorknob.

EVERYONE. WAIT!

DORIS. My special red lipstick!
She remembers just in time to wipe it off with tissue just as the door opens / and there

GRANDMOTHER. *(overlapping at "/")* And there is Grandmother, there is her same old grandma not suspecting a thing.

DORIS. Grandma.
GRANDMOTHER. Doris.
DORIS. *(it sounds funny now)* Doris.
GRANDMOTHER. You look flushed.
DORIS. Cold out there.
GRANDMOTHER. *(shaking her head)* Who ever saw a black girl turn pink.
DORIS. *(attitude)* You did, I guess.
GRANDMOTHER. Where do you think you're going?
DORIS. Bandstand is on.
GRANDMOTHER. Not 'til you water my zinnias it isn't. They're parched.
DORIS. *(quiet, almost to herself)* I know how they feel.
GRANDMOTHER. *(but Grandma notices)* You got a fire under your skin, poor girl. Just like your mom did.
DORIS. Not like her, like me.
GRANDMOTHER. Doris!
DORIS. Now on, you can call me Darlene.

Scene Five

DORIS. Vic Watts spares no expense on Darlene's first single.

VIC WATTS. Give me a hundred violins, Barry. Gimme a millionteen tubas. Electric harpsichords. Little combo of Romanian gypsies for the bridge. Get those gypsies on a plane and bring them here. I want a wall of sound for our girl Darlene. I want ears bleeding. I want hearts bleeding. I want little teenage hearts hemorrhaging into the radio all across our great nation!

DORIS. The lyrics prove to be a problem.

VIC WATTS. It's not rocket science, Darlene.
"Shoppa loppa shoop shoop.
He's sure the boy for me."

DORIS. "Shoppa loppa shoop shoop." "Shoopa loopa shop shop."
What's the difference, it's all stupid.

VIC WATTS. Respect, Darlene. There is a kind of genius in the stupidity of pop, Darlene, and we must respect that or we'll be out on the street with Nat King Whatshisname and all the fossils of yesteryear.

DORIS. There are three other girls in the group, but only Doris sits in the control room with Vic.
She feels a little thrill when she sees the envy in their faces.

VIC WATTS *(putting headphones on her head)* **Listen to this playback, baby.**

DORIS. Sometimes hers is the only voice that makes it on the record.

(Together with a recording of herself:)

Herself repeated many times over.

(Together with ten recordings of herself:)

A chorus of Doris.

VIC WATTS. One more take for me, Baby. Can you do that for me?

DORIS. I'm tired, Vic.
VIC WATTS. *(smooth)* **Tired's what happens when you do your thing, Baby.**
DORIS. He touches her knee.
VIC WATTS. **Baby?**
DORIS. And she relents.
VIC WATTS. *(shouting off)* **Take forty-seven, boys!**

(We hear the rhythm track start up, moving straight into:)

Scene Six

DORIS. *(into the mic)* Doris's voice starts in her diaphragm, passes through her larynx, travels into the microphone, through time, and out the woofers and tweeters of the future into the ears of a Young Man with a heartache, who wonders:

YOUNG MAN. What is it about these dilemmas that captivate his contemporary heart?

Tommy's from the wrong side of the tracks, Brenda wasn't invited to the party...

How do these things put a lump in his cynical twenty-first century throat?

DORIS. *(looking at him)* The Young Man is sixteen and he lives at the edge of a big city where girl groups are old news.

YOUNG MAN. *(not looking at her)* But he shuts his bedroom door and plays Darlene's songs like they're brand-new.

DORIS. Why is she his favorite? If he had the words, the Young Man might say:

YOUNG MAN. What I love about her voice is its very lack of experience. Pure and clear, it functions as a girlish replacement for my own, less speakable desires.

DORIS. *(their eyes meet for the first time)* But he doesn't have the words, not yet.

Scene Seven

(Under the following, a not-very-soulful late '50s/early '60s song. Something with Doris Day would be good. Distant and tinny, as if over the radio.)

GRANDMOTHER. Doris fixes the big bow on her prom dress while her date sits downstairs with Grandma.

(The Ludwig actor plays her Prom Date, a nerd.)

PROM DATE. I know all the latest dances. I know the Frug, the Swim, the Mashed Potato, the Green Tomato, the Phat Phatoozie, the Special Sauce. I know the Locomotion, I know the Commotion. I know the Five Figure Promotion. Your daughter will have a good time tonight.

GRANDMOTHER. Doris is my granddaughter.

PROM DATE. Of course she is. Just you look so young. I can't believe you're a grandma.

GRANDMOTHER. *(steely)* Grandmother doesn't say anything.

PROM DATE. The cherry phosphates fizz in front of them, on coasters.

GRANDMOTHER. Would I know your family, Steven? Are they churchgoers?

DORIS. Doris descends, just in time, looking like a fancy cake.

PROM DATE. Darlene, wow.

DORIS. Hi Steven.

PROM DATE. Still can't believe you're going to your own prom, a big success like you.

DORIS. I'm just Doris, Steven. Doris from homeroom.

GRANDMOTHER. Yesterday she was Darlene.

DORIS *(to Steven, ignoring Grandmother)* Whenever I walk into that school I feel like Doris again.

PROM DATE. *(playful)* Well, I got a corsage here for Darlene.

(Suddenly, the song she recorded with Vic comes on the radio. After the earlier song, it sounds comparatively expansive and soulful. Grandmother turns in the direction of the sound. Doris is spellbound.)

GRANDMOTHER. Good grief, Doris, is that you?

DORIS. The first time she ever heard herself on the radio.

GRANDMOTHER. Is that Wagner he has you singing?

DORIS. And she likes what she hears.

GRANDMOTHER. Wagner with tom-toms?

DORIS. Mr. Watts says it's public domain, so.

GRANDMOTHER. It's filthy music.

PROM DATE. *(suddenly interested)* **Yeah?**

DORIS. Ten years later, Doris will remember the first time she heard her own voice.

GRANDMOTHER. Ten years later, Grandmother is dead and the song can't hurt her any more.

PROM DATE. Ten years later, Steven still has the corsage he gave her, mummified in a little glass box.

DORIS. But here in the present, there's no time for reflection. Here in the present, everything starts to happen very fast.

VIC WATTS. *(off)* **Show me the Billboards, Louie.**

(Light shifts.)

DORIS. The single tops the Pop charts for two weeks

VIC WATTS. *(walking on with the billboard charts)* **Five weeks on the R&B.**

DORIS. Doris barely goes to high school any more.

VIC WATTS. Vic signs her permission slips.

DORIS. Instead of French, she studies how to talk to the press.

VIC WATTS. She is a quick study.

(Light shifts.)

DORIS. *(as if to the press)* **I am so privileged to be in this business. I thank God every day.**

I thank God and Mr. Vic Watts for showing me the power of music.

VIC WATTS. Ladies and Gentlemen, they're all ready to do their thing. Introducing Darlene and the Daybreakers!

(Doris turns to look at Vic and the song starts. We hear Wagner's "Liebestod" completely orchestrated like a '60s girl group song. Tom tom drums, tambourines, hand-claps, and Doris:)

DORIS. *(singing)* Do you hear that song
When he walks by?
Makes me sing
When he looks in my eyes…

Scene Eight

(The song fades down and we hear **WAGNER** *singing the same melody in an unsteady baritone. King Ludwig watches, rapt.)*

VIC WATTS. Before the song was Vic's hit single,
it was notes from the pen of an even more difficult genius.

DORIS. *(pronouncing it very wrong)* Richard Wagner

VIC WATTS. *(pronouncing it sort of wrong)* Richard Wagner

RICHARD WAGNER. *(pronouncing it perfectly, as if correcting them)* Richard Wagner sings the *Liebestod* for the first time in an unsteady baritone. He struggles to decipher his own mad scratchings.

LUDWIG. The young King Ludwig II watches. His courtiers try to ignore the pheasant waiting for them, fragrant, in the banquet room.

WAGNER. It occurs to Wagner that he is singing, quite literally, for his supper.

LUDWIG. The great man looks up from the page for a moment to explain: Isolde dies of love.

WAGNER. In death she finds release, at last, like an orgasm.

LUDWIG. The eighteen-year-old monarch looks at his feet and blushes.

WAGNER. I'm sure you have heard the French term "*petit mort.*" Well this is a *grand mort*.

LUDWIG. Ludwig II rushes out to the terrace.
He mops his brow,
He breathes the night air,
He counts the swans in his manmade pond,
He reminds himself: **You are *king*.**

WAGNER. My king—

LUDWIG. The great man seems almost vulnerable, asking:

WAGNER. My king, did you not enjoy the performance?

LUDWIG. On the contrary—

I found myself so overwhelmed by its beauty that I could not bear to stay.
WAGNER. And something unheard of: Wagner blushes back.
LUDWIG. They stay on the terrace together, awake with the night air.
WAGNER. **My kindred,**
LUDWIG. Wagner says, touching him on the shoulder.
WAGNER. **My young kindred, who has never known love, but can recognize its notes. You will be a true lover of the arts.**
LUDWIG. And, like a fairy tale, Ludwig waves his hand and brushes away Wagner's debt.
WAGNER. They go inside and eat the pheasant.
LUDWIG. (Which is really a pheasant stuffed with a goose stuffed with a guinea hen stuffed with a quince.)
WAGNER. **You live well, my friend. Very well indeed.**

Scene Nine

DORIS. Before she can even enjoy her number-one hit, Vic brings Doris a new song.

VIC WATTS. I wrote it for you, Baby.

DORIS. *(looking down at the page)* Doris reads the simple lyrics about a black girl with straight hair. Pretty black girl with white-girl hair and the guy who makes her want to sing, every time she looks in his dark glasses. *(Looking at Vic now.)* And she thinks: This sure sounds familiar.

VIC WATTS. Whaddaya think?

DORIS. How come it's the same.

VIC WATTS. What do you mean it's the same?

DORIS. All your songs got the same story. The girl is into a guy who everybody thinks is no good, but she can see on the inside he's really solid gold.

VIC WATTS. See, Darlene, every pop song is a little bitty drama and you only have 2.5 minutes to get through both acts. You got your conflict: The guy's no good. You got your resolution: Actually he's pretty good. See how that works?

DORIS. I just thought maybe there's a reason you like to write about the guy nobody likes. *(Sly.)* **I thought maybe you know that guy.**

VIC WATTS. *(looking at her)* And Vic thinks for the first time: Maybe this is a prize worth fighting for.

DORIS. *(looking at him)* And Doris thinks for the first time: Maybe he doesn't know how to win me.

VIC WATTS. Tell me about your Mom and Dad. You never talk about yourself.

DORIS. Not much to tell.

VIC WATTS. Then it won't take long.

DORIS. He was an exchange student. I guess nobody in France told him he wasn't supposed to get with a black girl. They were real young. And then they had me and I could never figure out *what* I was. Straight hair from Dad, and skin that tells you what I'm thinking behind it.

VIC WATTS. Oh yeah?
DORIS. I mean, the way I blush…when I'm nervous.
VIC WATTS. You're blushing right now.
DORIS. And Doris blushes even more.
VIC WATTS. Whatta you got to be nervous about anyway?

(She leans in and kisses him.)

VIC WATTS. The guy's supposed to kiss the girl.
DORIS. This isn't one of your love songs.
VIC WATTS. Maybe it is, Baby.

(As he kisses her back, the dark recording studio floats in.)

VIC WATTS. Easy on the mike, now. You're not Kate Smith singing the goddamn national anthem.
DORIS. Where's everybody else?
VIC WATTS. *(handing her headphones)* They'll be right there in your ear.
I laid them all down yesterday, so you can sing it just for me.
DORIS. There in the dark, all Doris can see is her own reflection, suspended over him, in the glass of the recording booth.
VIC WATTS. Then Vic flips a switch, and it's like he's playing a hundred violins straight into her head.

(Pause. We don't hear the music at first, only Doris does – but we can see that there's music in her head.)

(Doris starts to sing into the mic, straight to Vic. Her voice sounds acoustically vibrant, relaxed. He watches her, unblinking. The music starts to rise up, near the end, so that we hear what she's hearing.)

DORIS. *(rhythmically spoken intro:)*
They say he's too cool to love me right
They say he acts like the prince of night
But if they could look in his eyes, they'd see
Oh gosh, oh golly, that boy loves me.

(Singing now:)

'Guess he likes the way I do my hair
When he holds my hand the other girls stare
But I don't really care,
No-whoa-whoa-whoa-whoa-whoa
No I don't really care,
Whoa-whoa-whoa-whoa
Whoa-whoa-whoa-whoa-whoa-whoa.
I don't really care,
Everything around me fades
'Cuz I'm too busy staring
Into his deep, dark shades.
I can see our future,
I know I know I know we got it made
Yeah the future is ours now—

(She stops singing, but the backing track continues, the melody soaring.)

DORIS. Sorry.

VIC WATTS. Why'd you stop? Don't it feel good?

DORIS. "The future is ours." Just – sounds a little cocky is all.

VIC WATTS. Sounds pretty goddamn good is what it sounds.

(During the following, Vic takes her face in his hands.)

DORIS. She doesn't tell Vic the real reason she stopped: She can feel his power, and she can feel her own power, and it's lifting her up so high she's scared to look down.

(The music continues into:)

Scene Ten

YOUNG MAN. The Young Man walks into class with Darlene in his ears.

(We hear the song, faint now, as if it's bleeding out of the Young Man's headphones.)

MR. CAMPANI. The first day of school, and the new teacher tells him to take off his headphones.

(The song suddenly goes out.)

YOUNG MAN. This is Music Appreciation, isn't it?

MR. CAMPANI. *(not unkind)* **You'll appreciate the music I choose, when I choose.**

YOUNG MAN. The new teacher, Mr. Campani, is different. The students are scandalized by his pink bowtie.

MR. CAMPANI. Mr. Campani wears argyle socks and does not slouch.

YOUNG MAN. Mr. Campani does not say "doesn't." He says "does not."

You can see your reflection in his shoes.

MR. CAMPANI. He looks like he came into this world clean and he stayed that way.

YOUNG MAN. The boys in the back row lock eyes with one another, as if to say:

EVERYONE. *(as boys)* **"I know what he is."**

MR. CAMPANI. Mr. Campani is flamboyant.

YOUNG MAN. But Mr. Campani is *shrewdly* flamboyant: not a body flapping against all social codes, but a body that knows punctuation. *(We see the following:)* His wrist flies to his brow to indicate the hot sufferings of Werther; two fingers at his throat for consumptive Violetta, her head voice resurrected for one last hurrah. He acts out all the great opera scenes for us. But although he says

MR. CAMPANI. *(as if to students)* **I was once a singer**

YOUNG MAN. ...He never sings us a note.

MR. CAMPANI. At first I was scared of opera, like you

YOUNG MAN. He says, seeming to read our thoughts.

MR. CAMPANI. But when I saw Wagner's *Götterdämmerung*, I was so overwhelmed with emotion that I ran up the aisle and vomited in the lobby, right there on the red carpet.

YOUNG MAN. The teacher looks him straight in the eye, as though recognizing him for who he is: A romantic, a kindred upchucker, a queer.

MR. CAMPANI. Have any of you ever felt something like that, watching a performance?

YOUNG MAN. The Young Man looks down at his college-rule paper and blushes.

MR. CAMPANI. *(looking straight at the Young Man)* **Anyone?**

Scene Eleven

(We hear a talk show jingle. Rising chimes.)

VIC WATTS. Vic goes on a TV talk show with a man who talks even faster than him.

TALK SHOW HOST. In case you just tuned in, we've been talking to Detroit's boy blunder, record producer Vic Watts. That's right, the whiz-kid himself, here with his canary of the moment, the lovely Miss Darlene DuPont.

DORIS. Doris sits there thinking "Canaries don't sing as good as nightingales."

VIC WATTS. Thanks for having us, Stu.

DORIS. "Canaries just look pretty and die fast."

TALK SHOW HOST. Vic, I want the folks out there in teevee land to get a taste of that crazy ear candy you're feeding the kids these days.

VIC WATTS. It's your show, Stu.

TALK SHOW HOST. If I may read a quick sample:

(He puts on spectacles, theatrically.)

I believe this is Darlene's new single, "Gosh, Golly, He Loves Me."

(He reads very dry – no rhythm, no enthusiasm.)

"Guess he likes the way I do my hair.
When he holds my hand the other girls stare.
But I don't really care.
No whoa whoa whoa whoa whoa.
No, I don't really care.
Whoa whoa whoa whoa"—

DORIS. That's not how it sounds. Vic / makes it—

TALK SHOW HOST. Just a minute, sweetheart. It's not finished yet:

(Very official again:)

"Whoa whoa whoa whoa whoa whoa."

(He pauses importantly, looks at Vic.)

Now is that what you call a lyric, friend?

DORIS. Vic keeps it cool.

TALK SHOW HOST. The way you rhyme "whoa" with "whoa." You need a rhyming dictionary for that?

DORIS. Vic acts real cool, but Doris can see him dig his fingernails into the armchair 'till it leaves marks.

VIC WATTS. My songs are for dancing to. My songs are for falling in love to. They weren't meant for reading. You need the mix. You need the sweet sound machine. That's where I come in. So do me a favor and read that again, friend.

TALK SHOW HOST. Sorry?

VIC WATTS. Just read me that over from the start: "Guess he likes / The way I do my hair…"

(A reluctant pause.)

TALK SHOW HOST. "Guess he likes / The way I do my hair…"

VIC WATTS. Real nice, now just keep on keeping on like that.

(Talk Show Host repeats "Guess he likes / The way I do my hair" over and over.)

VIC WATTS. First off you add the rhythm track. Lay some hands on me baby.

(Doris starts to do hand claps.)

You got a sweet sound, Stu. Maybe you can come work for me when they cancel your show.

TALK SHOW HOST. *(uncomfortable)* Ha ha.

VIC WATTS. Once you lay that down, you add some more rhythm: Some tom toms, taste of Africa. *(Vic starts stomping his foot, in rhythm.)* The high hat, taste of Detroit. *(Doris makes the sound of a high hat.)* Now what we're gonna do is dub that together on the rhythm track and add a whole mess of chicks going:

VIC & DORIS.
> *Ooh Ooh, Ooh*
> *Ooh Ooh, Ooh*

VIC WATTS. **And to that you add some even messier chicks going:**

DORIS. *(more soulful)*
> *Ah Ah, Ah*
> *Ah Ah, Ah.*

> *(It has become a rousing, catchy tune now – majestic even:)*

DORIS.	VIC WATTS.	TALK SHOW HOST.
Ah Ah, Ah	*Ooh Ooh, Ooh*	*Guess he likes the*
Ah Ah, Ah	*Ooh Ooh, Ooh*	*way I do my hair*
Ah Ah, Ah	**Then you add a rainstorm,**	*Guess he likes the*
Ah Ah, Ah	**you add a glockenspiel, you**	*way I do my hair*
Ah Ah, Ah	**add a Javanese gamelan, you**	*Guess he likes the*
Ah Ah, Ah	**lay on a track of the goddamn**	*way I do my hair*
Ah Ah, Ah	**president going "Ich bin ein**	*Guess he likes—*
Ah Ah, Ah	**Berliner," you add some echo,**	
Ah Ah, Ah	**you add a hundred violins—**	

(Vic ends the "song" abruptly – dramatically, like a conductor ending Beethoven's Fifth.)

VIC WATTS. **And that, my friend, is a mother-fuckin' top-ten hit.**

> *(Looking out:)*

Can I say that on TV?

Scene Twelve

LUDWIG. King Ludwig moves Wagner to his dream palace in the mountains of Bavaria. Exotic birds festoon the trees; trained bears dance the latest steps in the great courtyard.

(Wagner ascends his tower for the first time.)

WAGNER. Wagner shuts himself in the tallest tower, where he begins his great *Ring* cycle.

LUDWIG. The friendship grows

WAGNER. The friendship verges on immoderacy.

LUDWIG. My lion of culture!

WAGNER. My speckled little rooster!

LUDWIG. My artist, my everything! Keeper of our future!

WAGNER. *(distastefully)* Ludwig's advisors...

(Doris plays **PFORDTEN** *and Vic Watts plays* **PFISTERMEISTER**. *Perhaps they each have a monocle in a different eye?)*

PFORDTEN. Pfordten

PFISTERMEISTER. Und Pfistermeister

WAGNER. ...Suspect that the King is growing too close to his resident genius.

LUDWIG. One night, at a state dinner, Wagner calls the King

WAGNER. *Mein junge,*

LUDWIG. *(moved)* "My boy."

PFISTERMEISTER. Old Pfistermeister narrows his eyes,

PFORDTEN. Old Pfordten tugs his mustache.

WAGNER. I meant no impudence, dear Sirs.

LUDWIG. ...While Ludwig pretends to be offended.

WAGNER. Whenever they aren't watching, Wagner puts his feet up on the damask as an army of servants takes down his demands.

LUDWIG. Whatever you desire, you shall have it!

(It would be good if the look of this evoked Vic's "I want hearts bleeding" speech.)

WAGNER. Give me a hundred piccolos. Give me a million-teen timpani.

LUDWIG. You ask too little!

WAGNER. Give me a hundred cannon and a hundred soldiers to light them. Horses with a sense of syncopation. I want war, I want Waterloo! They say when the smoke cleared on the battlefield, no one could tell who won. It will be the same when the music ends in the concert hall: no one will know who won!

Scene Thirteen

GRANDMOTHER. With her arthritis, it takes Doris's grandmother five minutes to walk out to the mailbox.

DORIS. She receives three bills, a coupon book, and a letter from High Wattage Studios, which she waits all morning to open.

VIC WATTS. (*speaking out; cordial in a slick way*)
Dear Mrs. Unsworth,

I am writing to congratulate you on raising such an exemplary granddaughter. It's clear that Darlene grew up with a true feminine ideal in the house. If you see her too seldom these days, it is simply because we are busy preparing her for the world: voice coaches, image advisers, posture consultants, stylists – all for one special young lady.

I thank you also for your letter dated June the 16th and respectfully disregard its rather quarrelsome tone as the well-intended concerns of a doting guardian. Darlene has also asked me to request that you stop attempting to contact her by telephone, as the rigors of her concert tour demand a stress-free environment. (*He holds up a photograph of Doris.*) *I am enclosing an auto-graphed 8 x 10 glossy of Darlene so that she can be right at home with you even while she's off on the ride of her life.*
Cordially,
Vic Watts
Dictated but not read.

GRANDMOTHER. Grandmother rips the letter into many small pieces.

DORIS. But she takes the glossy picture of Doris and puts it in a beautiful frame. She puts it where she'll see it every day and think:

GRANDMOTHER. Where'd he put the girl I knew?

(*Grandmother turns to see Doris, just as Doris turns away.*)

What tall tower has he trapped her in?

(*Light shifts. Continuous into:*)

Scene Fourteen

(Doris opens her eyes.)

VIC WATTS. **Happy birthday, Baby.**

DORIS. Vic gives Doris a Rolls for her sweet seventeen.

VIC WATTS. **Doris doesn't know what to say.**

DORIS. **Big red bow!**

VIC WATTS. **Who ever saw such a shiny thing, huh Baby?**

DORIS. **Like the flyest hearse I ever seen.**

VIC WATTS. **It's a funny way of thinking but yeah.**

DORIS. And he plants a minty

VIC WATTS. **Smooch**

DORIS. On her lips. She opens her eyes on the kiss and sees:

VIC WATTS. His eyes shut tight, just like when he listens to Wagner.

DORIS. And he seems like such a *boy* to her all of a sudden – this mad genius who everyone is scared of but not her. And she does the math in her head: Six weeks we've been together. Six weeks and three days.

VIC WATTS. **Baby.**

DORIS. **Mmnh?**

VIC WATTS. **Have a look in the glove compartment.**

DORIS. *(playful)* **What's in there – gloves?**

VIC WATTS. **Just look.**

DORIS. **A ring?**

VIC WATTS. **Happy birthday, Baby.**

DORIS. **A diamond – that means…**

VIC WATTS. **You're my sound, Baby. You're my *voice*.**

DORIS. *(embracing him)* **Oh Vic!**

VIC WATTS. **If it weren't for you, how would I say anything.**

DORIS. But right in the middle of their perfect moment, the Santa Ana wind sweeps through the Valley and catches Vic's toupee like a kite / and

VIC WATTS. And suddenly boy producer Vic Watts looks like he's right on the brink of a mid-life crisis.

DORIS. Vic?

VIC WATTS. *(recovering the toupee)* **Shit. Shit.**

DORIS. Vic, it's okay, my hair's falling out too.

VIC WATTS. *(the toupee back on now)* **I don't know what you're talking about.**

DORIS. *(going to him, tenderly)* **All the teasing, all that dye. It comes out on my comb every morning.**

VIC WATTS. What are you talking about?
I got a full head of hair.

DORIS. And for the first time since he gave her a new name, she sees: Vic's got a dangerous talent for making things so, just by saying it.

Scene Fifteen

WAGNER. I want a babbling brook to inspire me! I want a mountain to echo my notes back to me a hundredfold! I want a bird that sings Brahms in my ear 'til I sleep! No, Bach – I detest Brahms.

LUDWIG. Word spreads of Wagner's state-sponsored excess. The Munich journalists write:

(Campani and the Young Man play the JOURNALISTS.*)*

JOURNALIST 1. "Is he to forge Germany's bold new Art form in the flames of his own voluptuary?"

LUDWIG. And, more succinctly:

JOURNALIST 2. "Perhaps he will write his next opera on the virtues of effeminate decadenza?"

LUDWIG. And, most succinctly:

JOURNALISTS 1 & 2. "What ever happened to the *suffering* artist?"

WAGNER. And yet, even in this excess, Wagner is not happy.

LUDWIG. Even smothered in damask und dahlias?

WAGNER. Wagner is unhappy.

(Ludwig follows Wagner during the following:)

LUDWIG. Every day, he paces the vast wilds of the palace, looking for the inspiration they once offered. But he can no longer find the footprints of the gods. The birds in the thick Fir trees no longer possess the power of language. There are no more swords waiting to be named.

WAGNER. *(hushed, fearful)* There is no more music in his head.

(Continuous into:)

Scene Sixteen

VIC WATTS. Vic Watts likes it dead quiet.

DORIS. He builds a sound-proofed palace in Malibu and shuts Doris inside with him. The neighbors are scandalized by the pink stucco.

VIC WATTS. Songless birds festoon the trees. Bodyguards creep about the grounds, silently. Ten foot hedges keep the sunlight out.

DORIS. Doris doesn't sing anymore.

VIC WATTS. Sit back and enjoy retirement, Baby.

DORIS. She hasn't sung a note since that day at the studio Vic said:

(Light shifts. We hear a British Invasion-type song.)

VIC WATTS. Get a load of this.

DORIS. What is it?

VIC WATTS. The Wemberly Whigs.

DORIS. Wigs?

VIC WATTS. W-H-I-G. It's British or something. We'll give them a new name.

DORIS. You signed them?

VIC WATTS. They're *now*, they're new. They sound like... *new*.

DORIS. They sound like they're playing in a garage.

VIC WATTS. All the guys at the studio think it's ginchy.

DORIS. What's "ginchy?"

VIC WATTS. It's you about six months ago, Baby.

(Light shifts. Music out.)

DORIS. Now, instead of singing, she looks at her gold records hanging on the wall.

VIC WATTS. The only thing allowed to break the silence is Wagner's "Liebestod," which Vic plays to fall asleep.

(We start to hear the "Liebestod", needling quietly on a record player. The slow, languorous beginning.)

VIC WATTS. He sleeps soundly, dreaming of gunplay, and bodyguards, and Wagner.

DORIS. But Doris lies awake. *(Pause. The music.)*
Dead awake, at 2 am.

VIC WATTS. Finally she stumbles down Vic's seventy-six pink marble stairs to make herself a bologna sandwich.

DORIS. Quiet in this house, always so *quiet*.

VIC WATTS. The crumbs dropping down on Vic's ice-white baby grand.

DORIS. So quiet I want to break something just to hear the sound it makes.

VIC WATTS. Tomorrow he will ask her about the crumbs—

DORIS. But she doesn't care. Catching her reflection in the dark window, she asks it:
Had Vic Watts really believed he could make a star of her?

VIC WATTS. *(directly to her)* Had she really believed that he believed?

DORIS. Did love blind him so completely that he thought she could eclipse those other girls?
Sarah, with four and a half octaves; Martha, who could shape a song and make it hers.

VIC WATTS. Or had Vic *wanted* an ordinary voice? A mediocre talent that would depend on his decorations. *(Directly to her.)* A girl who would follow him anywhere, who would never leave.

DORIS. *(directly to him)* And so she leaves, just to prove him wrong. Middle of the night, with nothing but the clothes on her back.

VIC WATTS. She leaves the gold records on the wall:

DORIS. His name on them, not mine.

(We hear the "Liebestod", but it is slowly overwhelmed by the girl group version. Cross-fading so that we can hear how Vic Watts' song has lifted the melody.)

VIC WATTS. Vic sleeps right through it, his toupee on the nightstand.

DORIS. In the car, through the night, ninety miles an hour, all the way to Michigan,
Doris sings her voice out.

(All we hear is the girl group version now, continuous into:)

Scene Seventeen

YOUNG MAN. *(with headphones)* The Young Man plays Darlene so loud that the bells and locker slams fade away, and the dreaded high school becomes nothing but a music video for her song.

MR. CAMPANI. Sometimes, the Young Man follows Mr. Campani.

YOUNG MAN. He starts to take detours from his own dull day in order to walk ten paces behind his teacher:

(We see this.)

Down the long hall from Teacher's Lounge to First Period;

On to lunchtime and his cigarette breaks behind the stadium;

Down, after school, to the white Toyota Celica with the bumper sticker that reads:

MR. CAMPANI. "If it's not baroque, don't fix it."

YOUNG MAN. The Young Man is propelled, not deterred, by the possibility that his teacher will turn around and discover him there, twenty steps back.

(They both stop walking, a suspended moment. But Campani doesn't turn to look at him.)

MR. CAMPANI. But part of him knows: he'll have to risk more if he wants to be discovered.

(Light shifts.)

YOUNG MAN. For now, the Young Man must be satisfied with the lectures, when he closes his eyes and pretends Mr. Campani's words are just for him:

(Mr. Campani speaks out, in a light of his own. We are his students.)

MR. CAMPANI. Even when I'd just started singing, I could tell Wagner was different – before I read a single note.

At the top of his manuscripts, Johann Sebastian Bach wrote the initials "I.N.J." *In Nomine Jesu.* "In the name of Jesus," he wrote on the blank page, hopefully. *In Nomine Jesu*, as if to say: I am not making this to bring myself fame. This is dedicated to something outside of myself.

(We see Ludwig and Wagner now in another part of the stage.)

In giving myself over to divinity, I become it, it takes possession of me, it writes in my hand.

(Wagner lifts his quill.)

At the top of his manuscripts, Richard Wagner wrote, simply:

WAGNER. *(writing)*	MR. CAMPANI.
"Richard Wagner."	"Richard Wagner."

(Continuous into:)

Scene Eighteen

WAGNER. Wagner has written nothing on the page but his own name.

LUDWIG. Night after night like this. Ludwig sits at the dinner table alone, and the pheasant grows cold.

WAGNER. Wagner wets and rewets his pen. His candle has almost spent itself. He idly spins a globe, touching the purple paper of the African continent.

LUDWIG. He tears the hair from his head in salt-and-pepper pelts, contemplating the problem of Act Two:

WAGNER. **What would a dragon sing if it could sing?**

LUDWIG. As the composer retreats from the world, his patron rushes headlong into it: Hunting, horseback riding, all the pleasures of the sprawling estate.

(The Young Man plays the Stable Boy in the following.)

WAGNER. Wagner watches from the tower as Ludwig fastens a tiny bell around the stable boy's lovely neck.

LUDWIG. **A trinket for you, my boy. A token.**

STABLE BOY. The stable boy asks **what is it for?**

LUDWIG. **We would not want you taking any birds by surprise.**

STABLE BOY. They were students together, capturing bullfrogs and making them race. But now the young man kneels and kisses the emerald ring on his finger.

LUDWIG. Even as the boy takes him in his mouth, Ludwig cannot help but look to the highest window of the highest tower:

WAGNER. A light

LUDWIG. A candle

WAGNER *(looking down at his paper)* Wagner turns away from the window and the simpler pleasures it frames.

LUDWIG. The same old question on his lips:

WAGNER. **What would a dragon sing if it could sing?**

(Looking up)

Of course: It would sing fire!

(As Wagner starts to write furiously, we hear the orgasmic final minutes of the "Liebestod.")

LUDWIG. As the stable boy brings him to the edge of ecstasy, Ludwig leaves his slight body for a moment and flies up to that faraway window.

WAGNER. *Wer stort mir den Schlaf?* Wagner writes, his cursive unfurling like a skyfull of tails.

LUDWIG. Ludwig presses himself against the glass

WAGNER. But Wagner does not look up from his work.

(They are very close now, inches apart, but Wagner doesn't see him.)

LUDWIG. *(with great ardor)*
I experience life, but without perception.
You perceive life, but without experience.
Together, could we not be complete?

(Lights shift. The Stable Boy becomes the Young Man before our eyes.)

YOUNG MAN. Just as the King climaxes, the Young Man wakes up in his bed, his sheets sticky with the dream. A biography of Wagner lies open beside his pillow.

Scene Nineteen

(We still see the Young Man as Mr. Campani speaks out, in the classroom.)

MR. CAMPANI. Liebestod. *Liebe* and *Tod.* Love and death. Unified in one word, one action, one song. The long-delayed climax of Wagner's opera. The soprano has paced herself like a long-distance runner and, after four hours, she can finally spend the rest of her huge voice. "Do I alone hear this melody?" she sings.
Tristan lies dead at her feet, but she looks out into the audience and sees him resurrected. "Do I alone hear this melody?" The onlookers don't hear anything, and they pity her. But Wagner allows *us* to share in her madness. His orchestra plays the music in her head.
We all know what it's like to have a song in our head no one else can hear. To walk around all day humming a commercial jingle. To look at someone and hear a hundred violins.

(The school bell rings. Mr. Campani looks in its direction.)

Oh for some violins.

YOUNG MAN. And as the tide of students carries him to third period, the Young Man turns back and sees: Mr. Campani mouthing the words of the song.

WAGNER. But the song is not only in a classroom with linoleum floors. It is also in the palace of King Ludwig II, where Wagner sings, squinting at his own black markings.

VIC WATTS. It is also in the studio of Vic Watts, who takes Wagner's black markings and adds tom tom drums; he adds a tire chain, for rhythm; he adds four backup singers and he adds / Doris

DORIS. *(overlapping)* Doris turns the black markings back into a song that plays as she comes downstairs in a prom dress, smitten with her own perfected voice. / It plays

YOUNG MAN. *(overlapping)* It plays in the bedroom of a Young Man, who learns that this dumb pop song says more about desire than he knows how to say. The music teaches him *himself*. And the next time he is in Mr. Campani's class, the Young Man raises his hand to ask a question.

DORIS. *(looking at Vic)* **LUDWIG.** *(looking at Wagner)*
Some loves are on the Some loves are on the
verge of extinction. verge of extinction.

YOUNG MAN. *(looking at Campani)* Others are just beginning.

DORIS. And her song will outlast them all. It plays everywhere. It plays everywhere but the pink stucco palace of Vic Watts, who only listens to classical music, who plays the "Liebestod" over and over, with his eyes shut tight, probing it for the secrets of genius.

(A simultaneous event:

Ludwig watches Wagner, writing the song.

Doris watches Vic Watts, bent over his record player.

Lights slowly fade on everything but:

The Young Man, with his hand raised, watching Mr. Campani.)

YOUNG MAN. Mr. Campani?

(Mr. Campani turns and sees him. Violins. The final, shimmering bars of the "Liebestod." The song is all around them, and us.)

(Blackout.)

End of Act One

ACT TWO

Scene One

(The YOUNG MAN *raises his hand, just as he did at the end of Act One. But the classroom looks ordinary now, fluorescent. No violins.)*

YOUNG MAN. **Mr. Campani?**

MR. CAMPANI. **Yes, the young man with the hair in his eyes.**

YOUNG MAN. **Me?**

MR. CAMPANI. **I'm afraid I've forgotten your name.**

YOUNG MAN. **Jacob.**

MR. CAMPANI. *(looking straight at him)* Jacob wants to ask why Mr. Campani never sings for them, but he hasn't got the nerve.

YOUNG MAN. **I wondered, just— Did Wagner want to do that to people? I mean – Make them run up the aisle and throw up? Is that what he thought music is supposed to do?**

MR. CAMPANI. **I suspect, young man, that you already know the answer.**

YOUNG MAN. **Yes?**

MR. CAMPANI. **Any composer…any** *artist* **hopes to make the audience lose their lunch.**

Now did you have a real question for me?

YOUNG MAN. **How does it do that, the music?**

MR. CAMPANI. **I have devoted the last twenty-five years to the study of opera,**

and truly I do not know.

Scene Two

LUDWIG. Winter, and Ludwig races across the snow on a crystal-spangled sleigh shaped like the swan from *Lohengrin!*

WAGNER. While Wagner writes.

LUDWIG. Spring, and he hunts on a mountaintop fashioned tree-by-tree on the one in *Die Walküre!*

WAGNER. While Wagner writes.

LUDWIG. Summer, and he swims in a grotto fashioned rock-by-rock on the one from *Tannhauser!*

WAGNER. While Wagner writes.

LUDWIG. Ludwig has not only built a theater for Wagner's operas, he has rebuilt all Bavaria in their image. And himself, the heroic tenor!

WAGNER. Ludwig's advisors…

PFORDTEN. Pfordten

PFISTERMEISTER. Und Pfistermeister

WAGNER. …Are not amused.

PFORDTEN. *(simmering)* **He has rebuilt all Bavaria in Wagner's image.**

PFISTERMEISTER. *(simmering)* **The royal coffers are almost empty.**

WAGNER. While the king is busy with fantasies

PFORDTEN. Pfordten

PFISTERMEISTER. Und Pfistermeister

PFORDTEN & PFISTERMEISTER. Hatch an evil plan.

WAGNER. They begin to assemble a list of the King's eccentricities:

PFORDTEN. The King is so shy that, at state dinners, he has the musicians play so loudly that conversation is impossible.

PFISTERMEISTER. Every morning when he wakes, the King bows to the birds outside his window, and is heard to remark:

LUDWIG. Fill me with song, feathered friends.

WAGNER. One night, while Ludwig stares across the darkness at Wagner's tower, a letter is slipped under his door.

PFORDTEN & PFISTERMEISTER. My dear King,

LUDWIG. *(reading)* "Your Majesty's interest in music has devolved into an advanced stage of mental disorder, impacting Your Majesty's apprehension of reality. Suffering from such a disorder, freedom of action can no longer be allowed. Your Majesty is declared incapable of ruling, which incapacity will last for the length of Your Majesty's life."
Sincerely,"

PFORDTEN. Pfordten

PFISTERMEISTER. Und Pfistermeister.

(Ludwig drops the letter.)

LUDWIG. *(looking to Wagner in the tower)* There is only one place for him to run.

Scene Three

DORIS. Doris drives through the night to the house she grew up in.

GRANDMOTHER. Grandmother makes peppermint tea.

DORIS. **Oh Granny**

GRANDMOTHER. Grandmother dabs her runny mascara with a hankie.

DORIS. **It felt like I was drowning.**

GRANDMOTHER. Same one she used to dry her own daughter's tears, so many years ago.

DORIS. **We didn't even talk any more.**

GRANDMOTHER. **Well, you can talk soon.**

DORIS. **What do you mean?**

VIC WATTS. Just then, a pair of headlights shoots through the flowered curtains.

DORIS. **Who's here?**

GRANDMOTHER. *(with difficulty)* **I'm sorry, Doris.**

DORIS. **You told him I was coming?**

GRANDMOTHER. **He's your husband now. God knows I tried to stop things from going this far – but he's your husband now and you got to work things out, you're bound to him.**

DORIS. **What kind of caveman law is that?**

VIC WATTS. *(from outside)* **Darlene?**

GRANDMOTHER. **Your wedding vow, Doris.**

VIC WATTS. **Darlene!**

DORIS. *(shouting outside)* **How'd you get here so fast?**

VIC WATTS. **Private jet, baby.**

DORIS. **Well you can turn it right back around.**

VIC WATTS. **Open this door or I'm knocking it down.**

DORIS. **You couldn't knock out a tooth with that pansy-ass fist of yours!**

VIC WATTS. **Then I'll pay somebody to knock out your teeth, baby. Then you'll be too ugly to leave me.**

DORIS. *(turning back to Grandmother)* **Why are you making me do this alone?**

GRANDMOTHER. **When your own mom and dad left you alone, I was there for you Doris.**

VIC WATTS. **Darlene!**

DORIS. *(shouting outside)* **That's not my name!**

GRANDMOTHER. **One hit song, and you left this house and never turned back.**

VIC WATTS. **Darlene!**

GRANDMOTHER. **No one to get my groceries, no one to get my medicine.**

DORIS. **I fell in love.**

GRANDMOTHER. **With him? Or with what he made you?**

DORIS. **With *him*.**

VIC WATTS. **Darlene!**

GRANDMOTHER. **I'm sorry, Doris. But you two gotta try and make music together somehow.**

VIC WATTS. **DARLENE!**

(We hear the first blast of the Vengeance Trio from Wagner's Götterdämmerung. Grandmother becomes Mr. Campani right before our eyes. Continuous into:)

Scene Four

MR. CAMPANI. *(imposing, as if to the students)* **Die Götterdämmerung. The only opera with *two* umlauts.**

YOUNG MAN. Mr. Campani takes the class on a field trip to the local opera house.

MR. CAMPANI. *Die Götterdämmerung.* **The most bladder-punishing of all operas, the first Act alone runs two and half hours. Even with a king's patronage, it took Wagner four years to finish.**

(In another part of the stage, we see Wagner composing at his desk:)

WAGNER. Dissonance: The strings at seconds and sevenths. The brass –.

(Wagner is not sure what to do next.)

MR. CAMPANI. Act Two ends with the hair-raising Vengeance Trio: Under the influence of a love potion, Siegfried has abandoned Brunnhilde; now the valkyrie plots her revenge, and the music shares her taste for blood. "So be it," she sings. "Let his death atone for the shame he has brought me!"

YOUNG MAN. Three minutes into the Vengeance Trio of Act Two, the Young Man wonders why his stomach hasn't demanded a mad dash up the aisle. Is he not a true opera lover like Mr. Campani?

MR. CAMPANI. The Young Man's eyes wander from the stage, off to:

YOUNG MAN. The chandeliers,
The fur coats

MR. CAMPANI. The *boys.*

WAGNER. A flurry of Accidentals from the brass, rupturing the major chord.

(Wagner is stuck again. He chews his pen, staring at the page.)

MR. CAMPANI. The first time the Young Man has seen any of these sturdy-named classmates in evening wear.

YOUNG MAN. Teddy Duncan, Kip Fairfax, Pace Morrison.

(Billy Zimmer is played by the Vic Watts actor.)

BILLY ZIMMER. Best of all is Billy Zimmer

YOUNG MAN. Immediately to his right, wearing a yellow tuxedo shirt with brave irony

MR. CAMPANI. The top two buttons left undone, seemingly out of oversight,
offering a glimpse of chest hair.

BILLY ZIMMER. (This is Billy Zimmer's third year as a sophomore.)

WAGNER. *(a breakthrough)*
The trumpets sound a broken chord.
The timpani wake with a rumble.

YOUNG MAN *(pulse racing, but he barely moves)*
Emboldened by the Vengeance Trio, the Young Man shifts his knee ever so slightly toward the knee of the excellent Billy Zimmer on his immediate right, thanking God for putting the two of them alphabetically together on Mr. Campani's alphabetically-determined seating chart—

(Suddenly slow, expansive.)

WAGNER. From the strings, an augmented fifth

MR. CAMPANI. For several seconds they are

YOUNG MAN. Knee to knee

WAGNER. The strings, plucking

BILLY ZIMMER. Trouser on trouser

WAGNER. The trumpets, double-tonguing

MR. CAMPANI. The Young Man holds his breath.

WAGNER. Addolorato?
Affretando!

YOUNG MAN. Aware all over his skin

WAGNER. Accelerando,
Accelerando,
Accelerando!

(The Young Man stands suddenly.)

MR. CAMPANI. …Until he dashes up the aisle, just in time to heave upon the lush red carpeting of the lobby.

(Continuous into:)

Scene Five

(The papers flying off Wagner's desk.)

WAGNER. Accelerando,
Accelerando!

LUDWIG. *(off)* **Maestro, are you in there?**

WAGNER. Reluctantly, Wagner looks up from his Vengeance Trio.

LUDWIG. **Open the door at once!**

WAGNER. The violins still ringing in his head.

LUDWIG. **Open this door – I command you!**

WAGNER. *(turning to see Ludwig)* **My King. Why do you visit my tower so late?**

LUDWIG. **Because I mean to throw myself from it.**

WAGNER. **Are you as mad as they say?**

LUDWIG. **They mean to take my music from me – they mean to take my life from me!**

WAGNER. **So you will take it first.**

LUDWIG. **There is no other course, old friend. Step aside.**

WAGNER. **Forgive me my King, but I will not.**

LUDWIG. **Why do you keep me from a glorious death?**

(Short pause. Then, with dawning horror:)

Is it because I am your bank?

WAGNER. **My king, no –**

LUDWIG. **You would not want to lose your satin curtains, your dressing gowns.**

WAGNER. **I would not want to lose my greatest *listener.***

LUDWIG. *(moved)* **Take heart, old friend. Your music will surround me in the next world.**

(Ludwig makes a dash for the window, but Wagner holds him back.)

WAGNER. And Wagner sees: He is the author of the boy's madness.

LUDWIG. **Why do you block my way? Do you not believe in the everlasting soul?**

WAGNER. I don't know, my boy.

No one knows what kind of music waits for us after death.

LUDWIG. *(dumbfounded)* But...in *Parsifal*, the soul flies up on the wings of a dove. In *Lohengrin*, the swan rises from the lake. Brunnhilde leaps into the fire and the world is born anew!

WAGNER. *(touching Ludwig on the cheek)* My poor boy:

You merely fund my operas, you are not a character in them.

LUDWIG. For Ludwig, it is the ultimate betrayal.

(Light rises on Mr. Campani, speaking out:)

MR. CAMPANI. ...And when Pfordten and Pfistermeister arrived to take the young king to the asylum, he did nothing to resist.

WAGNER. My boy...

(Light remains on Wagner as he watches Ludwig leave.)

MR. CAMPANI. But Wagner must have realized that what he said was not altogether true... For it is often difficult to separate the music lover from the music.

(Continuous into:)

Scene Six

(Outside Grandmother's house. Vic is sitting on the sidewalk in a sharkskin suit, smoking a cigarette. A few hours later, and his rage is spent. Doris approaches.)

DORIS. All that huffing and puffing. Good thing we built this house outta brick.

(Vic is looking at his feet, deflated.)

You came all this way on that jet, you must have something to say.

VIC WATTS. Are you coming home or what?

(Pause. He realizes this isn't enough.)

I...want you to come back home please.

DORIS. I'm home right now.

VIC WATTS. Why you gotta act like that Darlene?

DORIS. What, like I got a head of my own?

VIC WATTS. I got you a walk-in closet. I got you a toy fucking poodle. You want a kid or something? We could have some of those too.

DORIS. *(abrupt)* Why'd you stop making my songs?

VIC WATTS. They stopped selling.

DORIS. So that's all it was about: how many people would buy it?

VIC WATTS. Or another way of saying it is: how many people would listen.

And nobody's listening to you any more Darlene. You got good diction, you got good moves. But four white boys from Liverpool have more soul than you.

DORIS *(shaken)* You...picked me, Vic. You made me believe I had it.

VIC WATTS. You didn't want it enough, Baby.

DORIS. *(it seems almost a surprise to her)* No. I guess I needed both of us wanting it.

VIC WATTS. Come on, Baby. Let's go home.

(Vic walks away. She doesn't move.)

MR. CAMPANI. Why is it difficult to separate the music from the music lover?

(We see Doris watching him go.)

The human body changes the very sound of an orchestra. When Wagner's great opera house at Bayreuth was completed, he tested the acoustics by filling all nine-hundred seats with soldiers from the local garrison. He could not be sure how his music would sound if there was a single empty seat. Think of that: A piece of music is really a duet between the instrument and the listener's body!

(Buzz. The class bell brings us back to fluorescent reality. Doris is gone.)

Ah, our own special brand of music.

(As if to departing students:)

Goodbye. Goodbye. Enjoy your freedom!

(The Young Man approaches with books in his arms.)

YOUNG MAN. Mr. Campani?

MR. CAMPANI. Ah, my young kindred, I enjoyed your paper very much. "Love as Malady" in *Tristan*, right?

YOUNG MAN. *(confidentially)* Mr. Campani, I did it.

MR. CAMPANI. You did what?

YOUNG MAN. I threw up at the *Ring*. Just like you!

MR. CAMPANI. That is…bracing news.

YOUNG MAN. I have to ask—

MR. CAMPANI. I hope that wasn't part of your research. Truth be told, I sometimes find your prose a bit confessional.

YOUNG MAN. I don't want to talk about the paper. I have to ask you something.

MR. CAMPANI. You're certain you want my advice – a grown man who wears a bow tie?

YOUNG MAN. I wanted to ask… *(Even more confidential)* What happens to people like me?

MR. CAMPANI. People like you.

YOUNG MAN. People like us.

MR. CAMPANI. *(amused by the euphemisms)* Music lovers?

YOUNG MAN. Yes.

MR. CAMPANI. You want me to tell you that a young suburban homosexual can grow up to be a beautiful swan.

YOUNG MAN. You sound so...

MR. CAMPANI. Glib? I'm sorry.

But tell me why someone so young should be so concerned about his future.

YOUNG MAN. Because it has to be better than here. I don't like myself here.

MR. CAMPANI. Maybe you should run away.

YOUNG MAN. What?

MR. CAMPANI. Maybe you should change your name.

YOUNG MAN. Is this, like, reverse psychology?

MR. CAMPANI. In opera, people are always running away to become themselves.

YOUNG MAN. And what happens to them then?

MR. CAMPANI. They get lost, and then they get more lost. Sometimes they follow talking birds. Sometimes they drink magic potions. Sometimes they leap into fire. But always, they look for love.

YOUNG MAN. And do they find it?

MR. CAMPANI. It depends on the composer.

YOUNG MAN. What do you mean?

MR. CAMPANI. My voice teacher liked to say: Italian music is like a kiss on the mouth. German music is a kiss on the forehead. French music is a kiss on the neck.

(Pause)

YOUNG MAN. What kind of music is this?

(Mr. Campani kisses him on the forehead.)

YOUNG MAN. *(disappointed)* People in Wagner kiss – I mean really kiss.

MR. CAMPANI. But a kiss in Wagner is never just a shabby little liplock. It is always a kind of transcendental...

YOUNG MAN. Consummation?

(Short pause)

YOUNG MAN. Aren't you attracted to me?

(Pause)

MR. CAMPANI. Yes.

YOUNG MAN. Don't you want to have sex with me?

(Pause)

MR. CAMPANI. Yes.

YOUNG MAN. Then why don't you?

MR. CAMPANI. My young kindred, are you so eager for your life to turn into an opera?

YOUNG MAN. Yes!

MR. CAMPANI. Then I have an operatic proposal for you: Go find someone your own age. Drink magic potions. Leap into fire. And after that, if I still hold some... interest for you, we can have another discussion.

YOUNG MAN. There's nobody here.

MR. CAMPANI. What about that Rimmer fellow?

YOUNG MAN. Billy Zimmer?

MR. CAMPANI. Yes of course, Zimmer.

YOUNG MAN. Billy Zimmer's a thug.

MR. CAMPANI. Some people find thuggery rather...magnetizing.

It's a mysterious but well-known phenomenon.

(Short pause)

YOUNG MAN. Mr. Campani?

MR. CAMPANI. Yes.

YOUNG MAN. What's your first name?

MR. CAMPANI. In opera, it is very bad form to answer that question.

YOUNG MAN. You're so weird.

(The Young Man runs off.)

MR. CAMPANI. And Mr. Campani, who is indeed weird, thinks of Wagner's Lohengrin, and Puccini's Calaf, and all the opera knights who keep their names secret. He thinks: It is always this secret that gives them their power.

Scene Seven

(We hear the "Liebestod," sounding less like fifty violins and more like a scratchy old record. Vic Watts is watching the record spin in a dark room.)

DORIS. Twenty years after the divorce,

VIC WATTS. Twenty years after the studio closed,

DORIS. Twenty years after she stopped answering to Darlene, Doris gets a call about a TV documentary.

VIC WATTS. It's the story of Vic Watts and his girl singers and they want her to spill it.

(Light shifts. Quite bright now, like klieg lights:)

And spill it she does.

DORIS. *(as if to the interviewer)* **I thought hey, great, we'll live together, we'll make records together. How could I have known everything would go dark? All of a sudden I married Vic and – *wham*.** *(She makes the gesture of doors slamming in her face.)* **Darkness.**

MAKEUP GIRL. The director whispers something to the make-up girl, who comes running to Doris.

DORIS. Doris asks her what she's up to with that powder puff.

(The Ludwig actress plays the Makeup Girl.)

MAKEUP GIRL. No one can see your pretty eyes under all that, Mrs. Watts.

DORIS. Miss Watts.

MAKEUP GIRL. No one can see your eyes under all that, Miss Watts.

DORIS. Sorry, honey. I haven't been on television since it turned color.

I guess I don't know what looks good.

MAKEUP GIRL. Miss Watts needs extra powder when they ask if she still sings.

DORIS. Never. Not even in the shower.

MAKEUP GIRL. And, as she holds still for the powder puff, she sees, over the make-up girl's shoulder...

VIC WATTS. *(Putting on the aviator glasses.)* …**A familiar face.**

DORIS. Still wearing those glasses, as if they'll ward off old age.

VIC WATTS. Twenty years.

DORIS. Twenty years.

(Doris and Vic look each other in the eye, for the first time in this scene.)

DORIS & VIC. They do not cross the room to say hello.

(But they don't look away.)

Scene Eight

MR. CAMPANI. *(out)* It might have seemed like magic – but the great innovation of Wagner's opera house was simply to turn out the lights. The emperors, kings, and queens used to go to the opera to be seen, splendid, in their box seats. Now, thanks to Wagner, they sit in the darkness with the rest of us.

Wagner did not want us to see the kings, or the conductor's wild arms, or even the orchestra, which he submerged for the first time, in a "pit." Which he did not call a "pit," as we do today, but rather a "mystic gulf" between audience and stage.

By snuffing the candles, by blacking out the orchestra, Wagner rendered the audience inseparable from the performance. Darkness, you see, is all the permission we need to lose ourselves. I think perhaps we are always looking for an excuse.

(In a dark part of the stage, the front seat of the Young Man's car. He is there with Billy Zimmer, each of them with a bottle of Michelob. Sounds of a nearby freeway.)

YOUNG MAN. '87 Thunderbird.

BILLY ZIMMER. "Ooh."

YOUNG MAN. All-pleather interiors.

BILLY ZIMMER. "Aah."

YOUNG MAN. Rusty hubcaps.

BILLY ZIMMER. *(re: the air freshener)* Smelling tree.

YOUNG MAN. It's new-car smell.

BILLY ZIMMER. Pretty butch, pretty Whitesnake video, remember? Redhead on the hood of that car, rolling around like some kinda fuck bunny. Just like this car, spitting image.

(Pause)

You ever have hair like those guys with the hair? Winger. *Kixx*.

YOUNG MAN. *(playing cool) Decades* before my time.

BILLY ZIMMER. Wall o' bangs, aqua net to the skies.

Hey, you trying to call me old?

YOUNG MAN. No no I just wanted to hear what you were like – growing up.

BILLY ZIMMER. Yah, hair was big the first time I was a sophomore. But our school's like a decade behind the rest of the world.

(Awkward pause)

So, what kind of music do *you* like.

YOUNG MAN. You know, the whole women-on-meds genre. Karen O. Cat Power.

BILLY ZIMMER. More like women *off* meds.

YOUNG MAN. And sometimes, you know, girl groups.

BILLY ZIMMER. Girl groups?

YOUNG MAN. Just sometimes.

BILLY ZIMMER. *("ew")* Like Destiny's Child?

YOUNG MAN. No. Wait.

BILLY ZIMMER. What?

YOUNG MAN. Just a second.

(The Young Man puts his headphones on Billy's head. We hear Doris's song.)

They're called Darlene and the Daybreakers.

There's four of them, but Darlene's the only voice on most of the tracks.

I copied it from 45s – they're pretty rare now.

BILLY ZIMMER. It's pretty okay. *(He takes off the headphones and the music goes out.)* Ironic-okay.

(Short pause.)

YOUNG MAN. It's good to see you out of school. Like we can be different, you know?

BILLY ZIMMER. Come on, you *love* school. I've seen you.

Did the Vulcan mindlink with that opera 'mo.

YOUNG MAN. I did not.

BILLY ZIMMER. *(mimicking Jacob)* "Why did Wagner want people to throw up?"

YOUNG MAN. It's just...his class is better than the others.

(Short pause.)

YOUNG MAN. I guess you know why I called you, why we're here.

BILLY ZIMMER. Cuz we haven't graduated to the back seat yet?

YOUNG MAN. I meant up here on the *hill* – don't be glib, I mean –

this is like the hardest thing I ever did.

BILLY ZIMMER. *(more flirty than mean)* What, you want some kinda reward?

YOUNG MAN. Um. No.

BILLY ZIMMER. Wait. Don't move.

(He kisses the Young Man. This lasts four or five seconds – not reticent.)

Surprise.

YOUNG MAN. *("wow")* Ha.

BILLY ZIMMER. Yeah. Yeah.

Before we do any more, maybe we should sort out the particulars.

YOUNG MAN. Huh?

BILLY ZIMMER. Finances?

YOUNG MAN. Finances.

BILLY ZIMMER. It's twenty if you're gonna blow me and more depending for what.

(Short pause.)

YOUNG MAN. You want me to pay you.

BILLY ZIMMER. The dads and granddads pay.

Spend time with a novice, you bet.

YOUNG MAN. I don't have any money.

I've got to – Just a second –

(The Young Man opens the car door to throw up.)

BILLY ZIMMER. Okay now that's gross.
  Okay. You're gonna be okay. Okay?
  When yer done with that you can drop me outside the movieplex.

(The Young Man gets up, woozy.)

YOUNG MAN. Sorry.

BILLY ZIMMER. You know you're not half ugly – might've discounted you.

YOUNG MAN. Why do you

BILLY ZIMMER. What.

YOUNG MAN. "Dads and granddads."

BILLY ZIMMER. Not like it's a *career*. But it's money, and it's not flipping burgers or four years in combat boots. TV's always telling you:

  (In the manner of an earnest talk show host, à la Ricki Lake:)

  "Don't debase yourself. Gotta respect yourself *Apply* yourself."

YOUNG MAN. So?

BILLY ZIMMER. So they just want to keep you from a good thing.

YOUNG MAN. This is a good thing?

BILLY ZIMMER. *(re: his prowess)* This thing
  is legendary.

(The Young Man counts the crumpled bills in his pocket.)

YOUNG MAN. I've got seven dollars. What's that get?

BILLY ZIMMER. Kiss goodbye?

YOUNG MAN. –.

BILLY ZIMMER. Hey hey, don't be so sensitive!
  Keep your seven bucks – I'll give you a virgin burn, free of charge.

YOUNG MAN. What's a virgin burn?

BILLY ZIMMER. I'll show you.
YOUNG MAN. No, I don't want to know.
BILLY ZIMMER. Whatever.
YOUNG MAN. I don't want to know.

(The Young Man starts the car.)

Scene Nine

(Back at the television studio. Doris and Vic as they were, eyeing each other across the room.)

DORIS. Pretty soon it's Vic's turn in the hot seat.

MAKEUP GIRL. *(powder-puffing Vic)* Mr. Watts has even more makeup on than Miss Watts.

DORIS. The interviewer lobs him some easy ones first.

VIC WATTS. *(as if to the interviewer)* **Sure I like today's music. Prince can write a song. Bananarama's got it. Name like Bananarama, you'd better goddamn have it.**

DORIS. But then she goes off the script.

VIC WATTS. The love of my life?
I thought we said nothing personal.

DORIS. But the interviewer leans forward in her chair.

VIC WATTS. The love of my life...

DORIS. And Doris holds her breath.

(Short pause.)

VIC WATTS. The music.

(Looking straight at Doris)

It was always the music.

MAKEUP GIRL. And then the strangest thing.

DORIS. Doris starts to sing.

VIC WATTS. After twenty years of

DORIS. Nothing

VIC WATTS. She opens her mouth

DORIS. And sings the song he wrote to make her love him.

(Under the following, we might hear an echo of the second single, "Gosh Golly He Loves Me." Not the vocal, but the rhythm track and melody.)

DORIS. And it's a little bit ugly
And a little bit pretty
And a little bit frail

And a little bit strong
And a little bit magic
Like waking up one day and learning you can shoot lasers out your eyes or lightning out your fingers.

VIC WATTS. And as producers and makeup girls swirl around her, Doris won't stop singing, as if to say:

**DORIS. It wasn't the music you loved. And it wasn't me.
It was something a little bit both.**

Scene Ten

(We see Wagner watching Ludwig leave, as before.)

LUDWIG. Three days later, they find Ludwig's body at the bottom of the lake where he counted swans and dreamed of enchanted swords.

WAGNER. No one knows what happened for certain.

LUDWIG. Some say he escaped the asylum and drowned himself. Others say he was murdered.

WAGNER. But Wagner knew better. Ludwig had always imagined himself as a character in *Lohengrin*, more than any of the other operas. It seems impossible that he could have entered the dark water that night without thinking of the final scene of *Lohengrin*.

(During the following, Ludwig walks into the lake and drowns. Serene, as if reassuring himself with an old bedtime story. We hear music from the final scene of "Lohengrin.")

LUDWIG. **Lohengrin recognizes the swan as the young man enchanted many years ago, prisoned in an animal's body.**

He loosens the chain round the swan's neck.

The swan sinks into the lake, and in its place appears a boy in shining silver.

Lohengrin lifts the boy from the water and places the crown on his head again, and he is silver.

(Continuous into:)

Scene Eleven

(The classroom.)

MR. CAMPANI. *(out)* Maybe Ludwig believed that he too would be lifted out of the lake, restored. This man who dedicated his life to making Wagner's fictions real. But as his lungs filled with water, the king must have known for the first time that music doesn't always tell the truth. One thing is for certain: Ludwig died of romanticism.

(The bell rings, loud. Light returns.)

He would not survive long at this school, that much I am sure of.

(The Young Man approaches Mr. Campani.)

MR. CAMPANI. Ah, young Master Jacob.

YOUNG MAN. It happened again.

MR. CAMPANI. Again?

YOUNG MAN. *(touching his stomach)* All over the car.

MR. CAMPANI. You must be a true music lover.

YOUNG MAN. Don't joke.

MR. CAMPANI. Have you considered Pepto Bismol?

YOUNG MAN. I said don't joke.

MR. CAMPANI. Yes of course – a budding aesthete couldn't be caught smiling.

YOUNG MAN. *("listen")* He wanted me to pay him.

MR. CAMPANI. Billy Zimmer? Oh dear. He's wilier than he looks.

Did you pay him then?

YOUNG MAN. What?

MR. CAMPANI. Did you go through with it?

YOUNG MAN. Are you kidding?

MR. CAMPANI. I thought you were looking for experience.

YOUNG MAN. That's sick, that's / sick—

MR. CAMPANI. No my kindred, just realistic.

YOUNG MAN. You're a bitter old man. Life has been disappointing to you and now you're trying to make me like you!

MR. CAMPANI. Ah, splendid: fifteen-year-old psychoanalysis.

YOUNG MAN. I'm *sixteen.*

(*Pause.*)

I thought you–
The last time, you said, we could have another discussion...

(*Pause.*)

MR. CAMPANI. I don't think that's a / good—

YOUNG MAN. You said that / we could—

MR. CAMPANI. I was mistaken.
Now, if you'll excuse me, I have thirty dispassionate papers on *Rigoletto* to grade.

(*Campani busies himself. A moment where the Young Man has nothing left to lose.*)

YOUNG MAN. Mr. Campani?
Why did you stop singing?

(*Mr. Campani is arrested by the question.*)

(*Doris appears. She watches the rest of the scene, unnoticed by the Young Man and Mr. Campani.*)

DORIS. Because I wasn't ever going to be great.

MR. CAMPANI. Because I wasn't ever going to be great.

YOUNG MAN. You mean you shouldn't do something unless you're great at it?

MR. CAMPANI. That's what I thought then. And you're right, I was...disappointed. (*With difficulty.*) Some voices grow, with every role, with every challenge. Mine did not. When I was your age I was at Juilliard and ten years later my career was over. But I already loved it too much.

(*Ludwig appears. He watches the rest of the scene, unnoticed.*)

YOUNG MAN. What do you mean?

LUDWIG. Once you let music take you over, you can never be cured.

MR. CAMPANI. Once you let music take you over, you can never be cured. So many things have happened to me since I gave up singing. New careers and new lovers, new cities. *(Re: his age.)* New lines. But I don't know if anything has compared to looking out into the dark, singing someone else's words to a roomful of strangers. I don't think I'll ever be that…important again.

(Wagner and Vic Watts approach from different directions.)

YOUNG MAN. *(to Campani)* I think you're important.

WAGNER. *(to Ludwig)*	VIC WATTS. *(to Doris)*
Maybe that's why it's so easy to hurt you.	Maybe that's why it's so easy to hurt you.

MR. CAMPANI. *(to Young Man)* Maybe that's why it's so easy to hurt you.

(Pause.)

YOUNG MAN. Would you sing for me?

MR. CAMPANI. Right here? Right now?

YOUNG MAN. Please.

MR. CAMPANI. It's not like riding a bicycle. The voice demands constant attention.

YOUNG MAN. What are you scared of?

MR. CAMPANI. What if nothing comes out?

DORIS. But after all those years, the urge to sing again is strong.

LUDWIG. And it is hard to disappoint the look in the eyes of his biggest fan.

WAGNER. And Mr. Campani plants his feet, and takes a deep breath, and starts to sing the *Liebestod* in a beautiful, unsteady baritone.

(Mr. Campani starts to sing. His voice is ragged now, but he still sings with great precision. And hints of the voice he once had.)

YOUNG MAN. The Young Man watches.

WAGNER. The way the older man's eyebrows reach for the high notes.

VIC WATTS. The way he rises up on the balls of his feet.

DORIS. This man whose shoes are always shined.

LUDWIG. Finally his body has lost some of its control.

WAGNER. It has become a servant to the music.

LUDWIG. And, as he listens to this song about a great love finally consummated, the Young Man wonders if his kiss will be returned.

DORIS. Part of him wants the song to last forever.

YOUNG MAN. *(looking at Mr. Campani)* Part of him wishes he never heard the song that got him into all this trouble.

(Light shifts. Continuous into:)

Scene Twelve

(Lights rise slowly on the record player that Doris brought on at the beginning of the play. A record spins on it, scratching softly. The end of the record, or the beginning.)

MR. CAMPANI. The *Liebestod* jumps back down Mr. Campani's throat and stays there until he is a young man with a great singing career ahead of him, and the song doesn't sound nearly as sad.

YOUNG MAN. The Young Man backs out of Mr. Campani's room and goes back to junior high. He plays Doris's song on his headphones, loud, hoping it will teach him something about love. But he no longer knows where the song came from.

DORIS. The song plays in discount stores and workout videos and on a TV documentary where Doris appears with words on the bottom of the screen to remind people who she is.

VIC WATTS. Before long, the song slips off the gold record on the wall in a quiet living room in Malibu. Skips off the record and climbs back into Doris's mouth / and

DORIS. And music fills the quiet house again. Doris backs up the aisle in a wedding dress and Vic takes the ring off her finger and her heart is unbroken.

VIC WATTS. The song she's sung so many times plays over the radio for the very first time, and the song climbs back up the microphone cord in Vic's studio, / and

DORIS. And the number nine bus takes Doris back to her grandmother. She grows smaller and smaller with every day, and eventually she grows so small that her mother and father take her back again.

VIC WATTS. And the *Liebestod* waits patiently all this time, black notes on paper. It sleeps on paper for a hundred years / until

LUDWIG. Until King Ludwig climbs out of the swan pond and shakes his long hair dry. The water exits his lungs and his lungs fill with air and the air carries the song out of his mouth / and

WAGNER. And into the mouth of Wagner, who sings it for the first time in an unsteady baritone while the courtiers think of the pheasant, fragrant, in the next room.

LUDWIG. The pond dries up. The swans fly back to their natural habitat. The pink marble climbs off its foundation and crawls back to a Venetian quarry, and the grass grows taller and taller.

WAGNER. Wagner forgets the name Ludwig and moves back to his family and destitution. The gold coins fly out of his purse, the fine silk falls off his body. But his pen moves faster with every day, and his ideas grow fresher, and his old body stands taller and taller.

LUDWIG. King Ludwig takes off his crown and forgets the name Wagner, and he is a young boy who dreams of swans and his heart is unbroken.

WAGNER. The black notes of the *Liebestod* skip off the paper and back into Wagner's head, where they wait to be written. But they don't wait for long. They fly out of his head and out into the world, where they become days he hasn't lived yet, and hearts he hasn't broken, and birdsong he hasn't heard: all the newborn, excited atoms of a song before the artist plucks it out of the air.

(Wagner's pen lifts off the paper and up into the air, where it pauses for an instant.

At the same instant, Doris lifts the needle off the record.

Blackout.)

End of Play

Also by Jordan Harrison...

AMAZONS AND THEIR MEN

Drama / 2m, 2f, / Interior

The Frau used to direct beautiful films for a fascist government. Now she's trying to make a film that's simply beautiful. The Frau casts herself in the lead role of the Amazon queen Penthesilea, who falls in love with Achilles on the battlefield of the Trojan War. She recruits a man from the Jewish ghetto to play her Achilles. Her own sister, a long-suffering extra, plays all the nameless Amazons killed in the background. With chariot crashes and adoring close-ups, it all has the makings of a glamorous war. But when telegrams start to arrive from the Minister of Propaganda, it becomes impossible for the Frau to ignore the real war outside her sound stage. A darkly comedic look at the role of artists during wartime, *AMAZONS AND THEIR MEN* is inspired by the life and work of Leni Riefenstahl.

"The life of Leni Riefenstahl... has been examined and critiqued aplenty, but rarely so entertainingly as in *AMAZONS AND THEIR MEN*, a brash play by Jordan Harrison."
- *New York Times*

" In a dramatic masterstroke, the playwright imagines Riefenstahl's film as it could have been..."
- *NY Press*

"Filled with dazzling wordplay, archaic vocabulary, and odd malapropisms, the theatrical worlds of Jordan Harrison lift language off the page and into three-dimensional space, creating a universe that is surreal and sublime, brainy and beautiful—and wholly his own."
- *Brooklyn Rail*

SAMUELFRENCH.COM